Contents

Visiting the Museum *by Bill Condon* . .
When a Dinosaur Dad Comes Home
   from Work *by Colin McNaughton* 3
Mr and Mrs Blob *by Marisa Horsford* 4
Spider *by June Crebbin* 5
Nobody from Nowhere *by Adrian Mitchell* 6
A Family Picnic *by Dick King-Smith* 10
Wanted! One Brave Owner *by Andrew Collett* 11
Ghost Eye *by Matthew Sweeney* 12
Butterfly *by Michael Harrison* 13
A Really Hot Meal *by Gavin Ewart* 14
Miss Antrobus *by Richard Edwards* 15
Meece *by Sam McBratney* 16
Film *by Roger McGough* 17
NoHaiku *by Adrian Henri* 18
Traffic Lights *by George Szirtes* 19
Fishing *by Gerard Benson* 20
There's an Old Town *By Brian Patten* 21
Robber J. Badguy *by Dennis Lee* 22
Index of poem features 24

Visiting the Museum

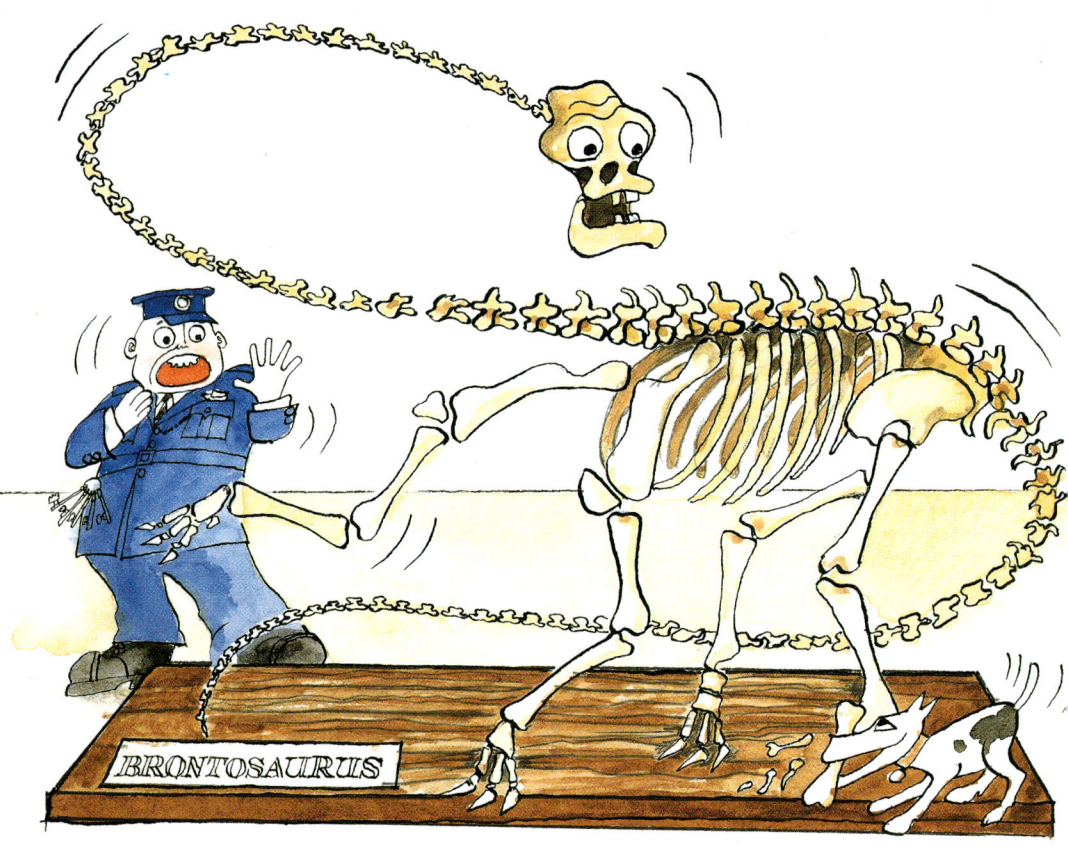

We tried hard to head him off
But alas he got there before us …

Never take a hungry dog
To see a brontosaurus.

Bill Condon

When a Dinosaur Dad Comes Home from Work

Be nice to Dad when he comes home
(Of course he'd never beat you!)
But if he's had a tiring day
He might just up and eat you!

Colin McNaughton

Mr and Mrs Blob

I was doing
some writing at school

When my pen
stopped working.

I figured that
It was on strike.

Then two BIG
BLOBS came out:

Mr Blob

Mrs Blob

Marisa Horsford

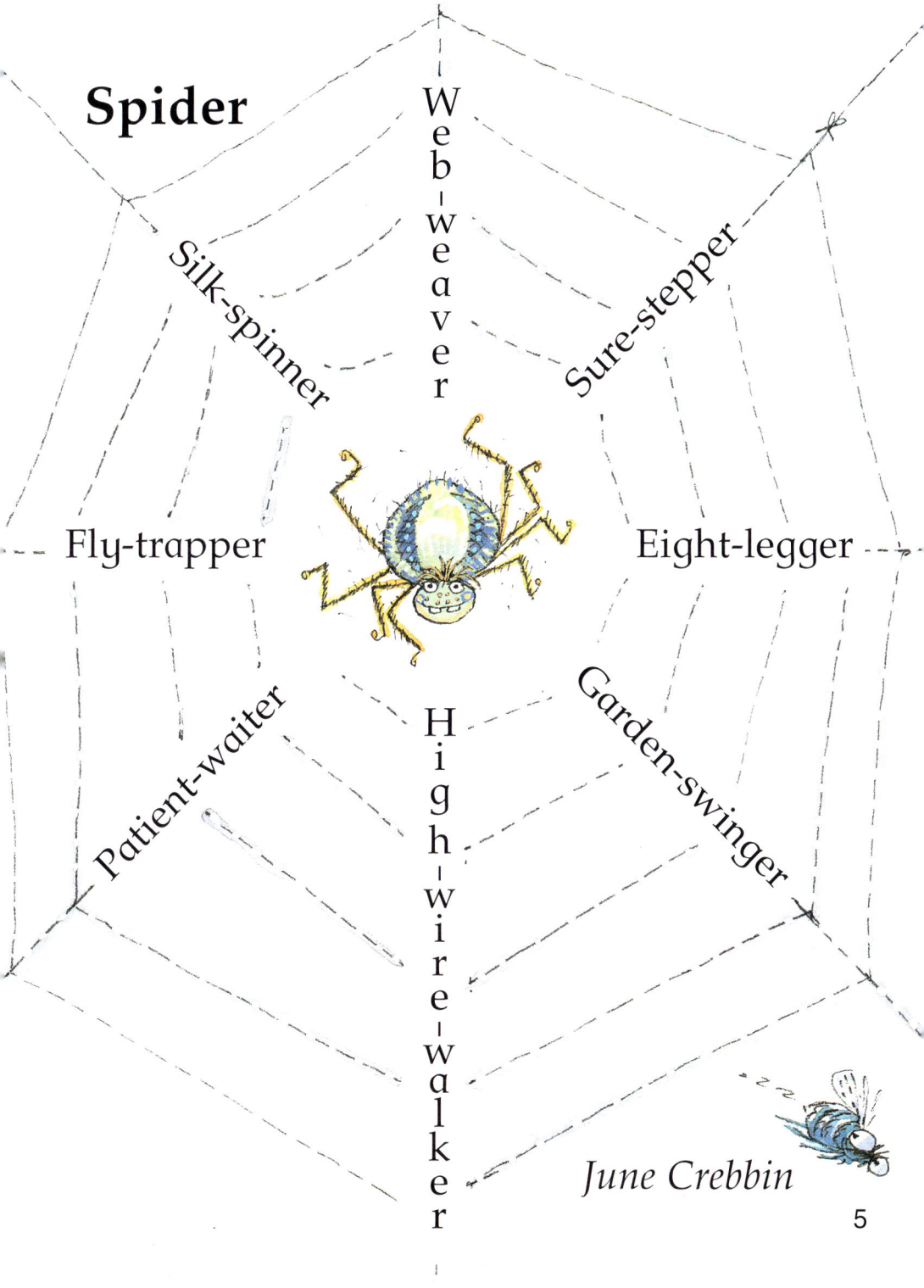

Nobody from Nowhere

The Nurse she said:
What you doing in bed?
I said: nothing.
The Matron came
And asked: What's your name?
I said: nobody.
The Student with his comb
Said: Where's your home?
I said: nowhere.
The Doctor prodded,
The Doctor nodded.
I heard the Doctor say:
Who are you anyway?
I said: nobody.

You see, I was feeling so miserable
I was trying to turn inviserable.
Then they gave me a pill and a
   big mug of tea
And I floated away on a blackcurrant sea
Up a cliff of cream buns
To a sky full of suns.

And I don't know how it happened
But I know I was rapping.
Yes flying over London,
With my pyjamas flapping.

I was munching marshmallows
In the marshes of Mars
And I whooshed through the
   Milky Way's
Sherbet of stars.

Then I was hopping on the Moon
With my galactic Mum
Till I tripped on some Krypton
And landed on my bum.

And my eyes began to open
And I heard the Nurse say:
You've had your operation –
How are you today?
Nobody from Nowhere,
Do you feel OK?

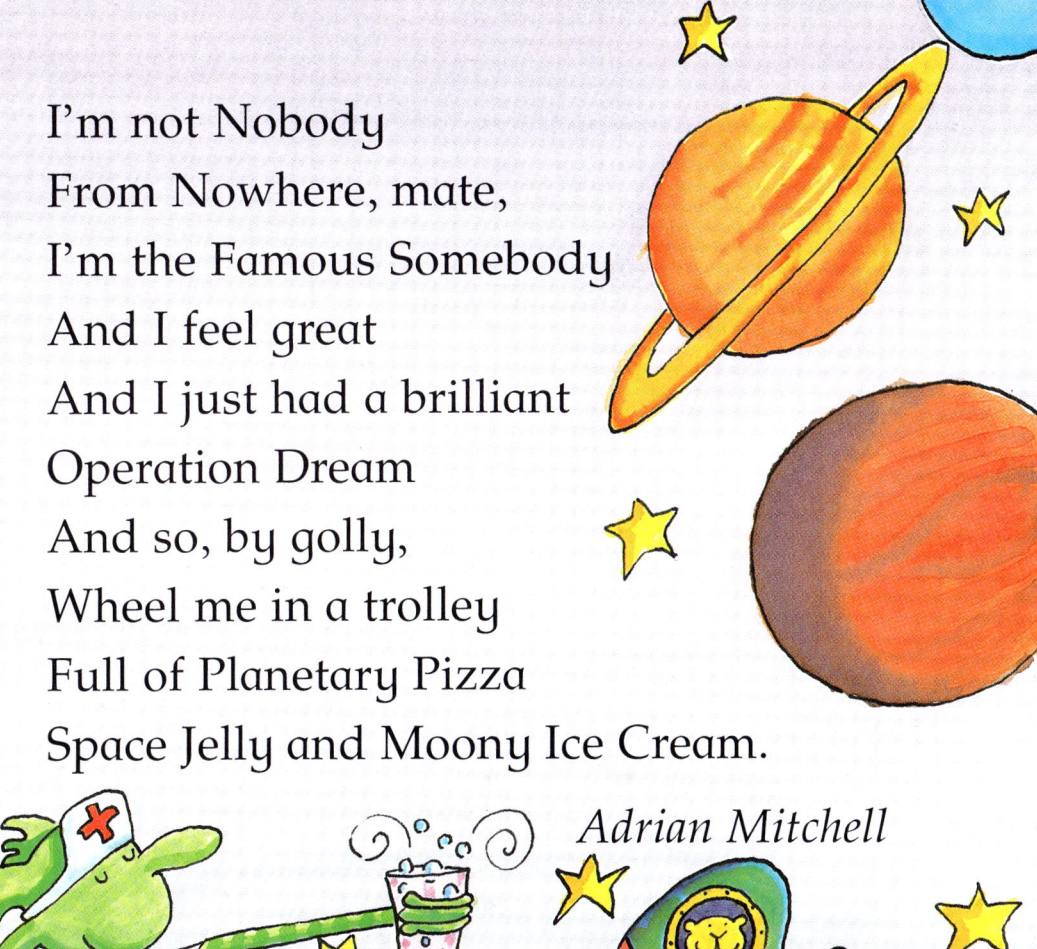

I'm not Nobody
From Nowhere, mate,
I'm the Famous Somebody
And I feel great
And I just had a brilliant
Operation Dream
And so, by golly,
Wheel me in a trolley
Full of Planetary Pizza
Space Jelly and Moony Ice Cream.

Adrian Mitchell

A Family Picnic

If you meet with a man-eating Tiger,
Don't think that it only eats men.
When it's polished off Dad, it'll start
  on your mother,
Your sister, your auntie, your new
  baby brother,
And shortly be hungry again.

For afters, it might manage you and
  your gran,
So don't think a man-eater only
  eats man.

*Dick
King-Smith*

Wanted! One Brave Owner

Wanted, one owner,
quiet and polite,
to look after me
daytime and night.

Someone to feed me
without being mean,
someone to keep me
tidy and clean.

Someone who'll let me
sleep in a chair,
someone who doesn't
easily scare.

So if you think
a tiger's for you,
just leave your name
when next at the zoo.

Thank You!

Andrew Collett

Ghost Eye

Mama, the ghost eye is here again –
all the way from the equator
where it lives in a dead seagull.
I'm taking my bed up to the attic
where I'll bolt myself in, Mama,
and I'm taking the robot dog with me
to guard me, my robot eye-eater.

Matthew Sweeney

Butterfly

Butterfly
Butterflies
Butterflown

Michael Harrison

A Really Hot Meal

A REALLY hot meal
Doesn't appeal
To a Seal.
Its favourite dish
Is very cold fish!

Gavin Ewart

Miss Antrobus

Why do you love your octopus,
Miss Antrobus, Miss Antrobus?
Why do you love your octopus,
Miss Antrobus, my dear?

I love my octopus because
It hugs me and it wriggles,
I love my octopus because
Its wriggles give me giggles,
I love my octopus because
It juggles jars of pickles,
I love my octopus because
It tickles, oh, it tickles!

Richard Edwards

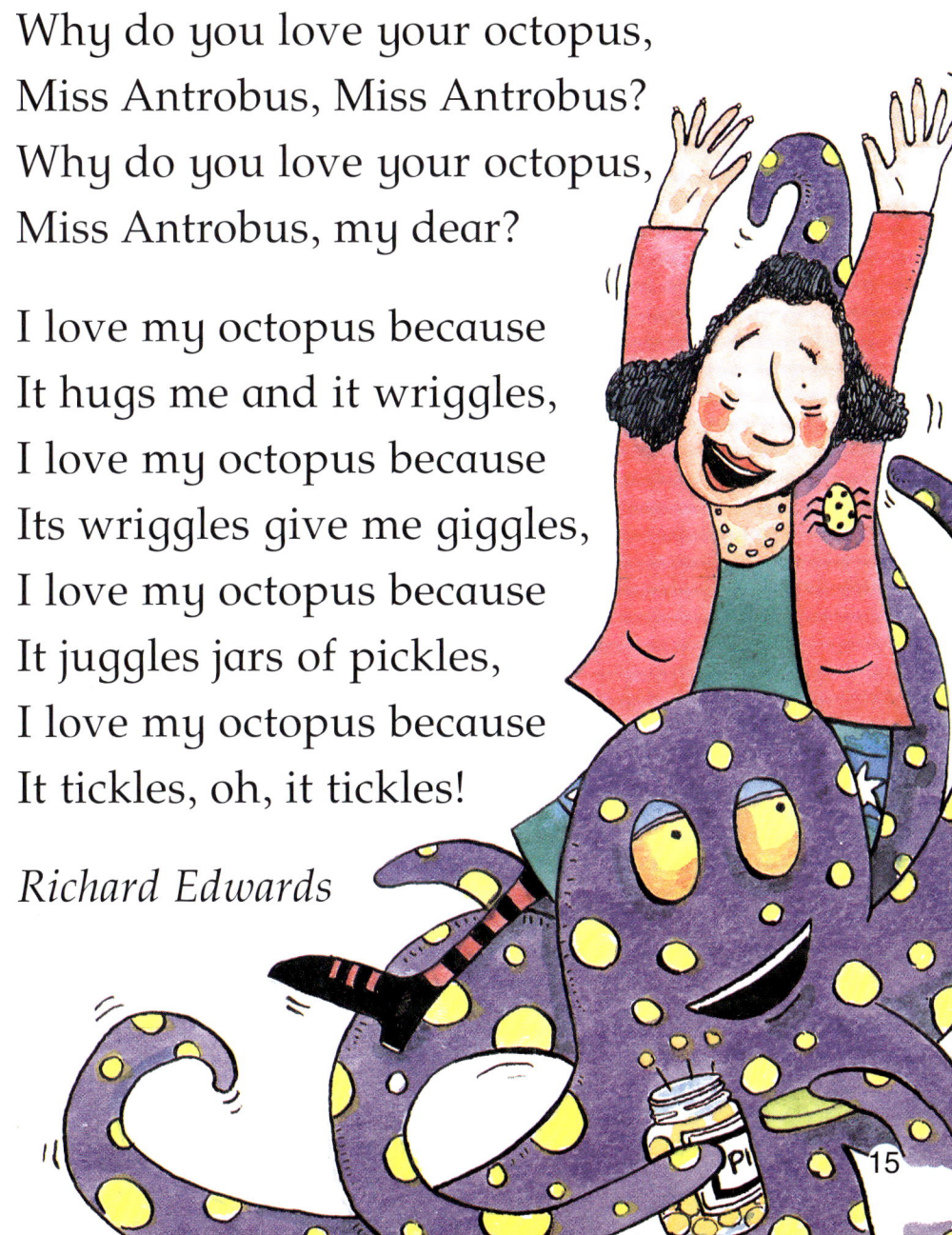

Meece

If mouses are mice,
and gooses are geese,
What excuses have mooses
for not being meece?

Sam McBratney

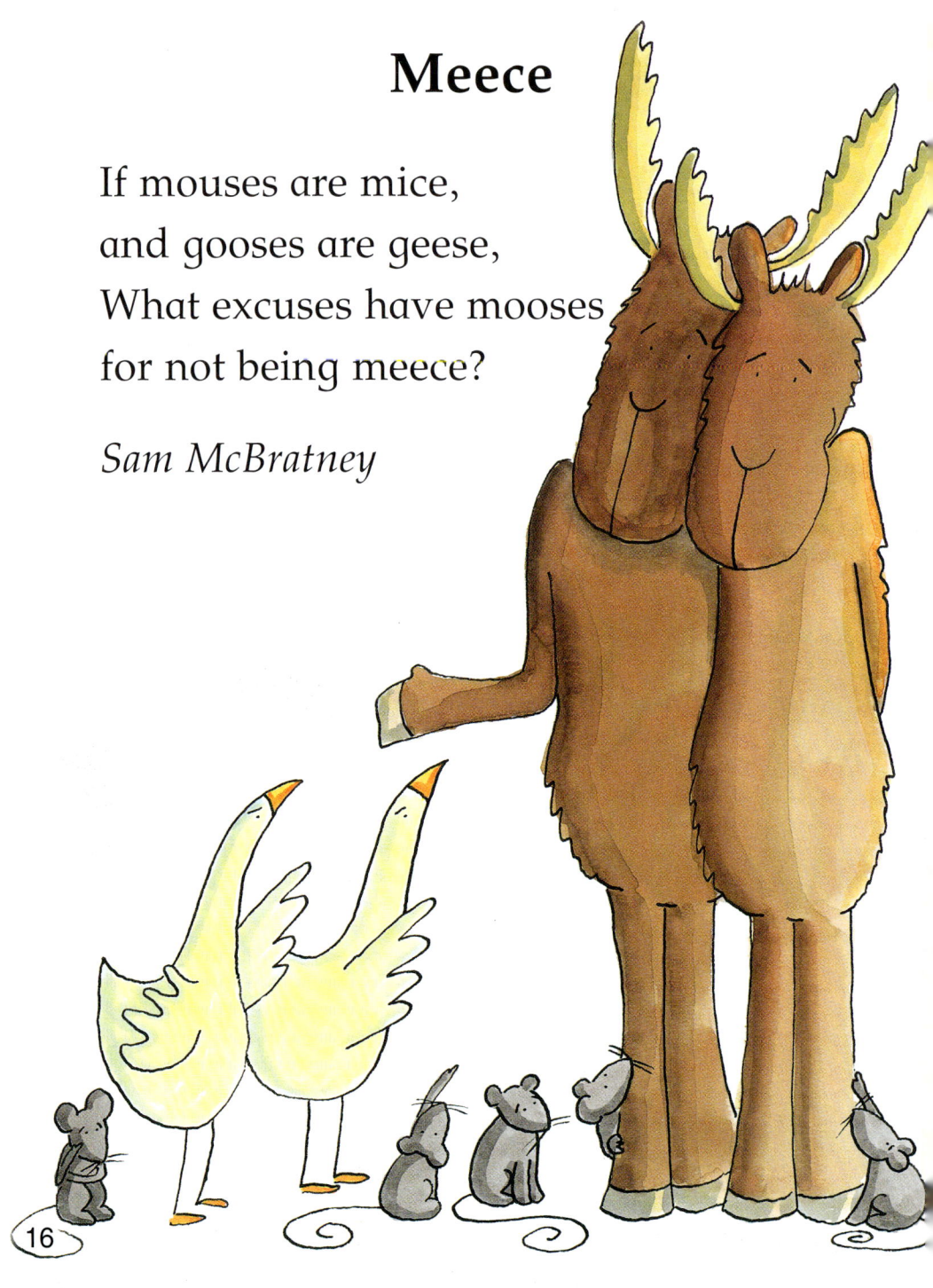

Film

Went to the cinema
Friday.
Tried to leave before
the end.

Couldn't get out.
It was a cling film.

Roger McGough

NoHaiku

I'm sorry to say
that I really don't feel like
a haiku today.

Adrian Henri

Traffic Lights

On the top sits fire,
In the middle gold
At the bottom grass.

At the top you stop
In the middle wait
And at the bottom, pass.

George Szirtes

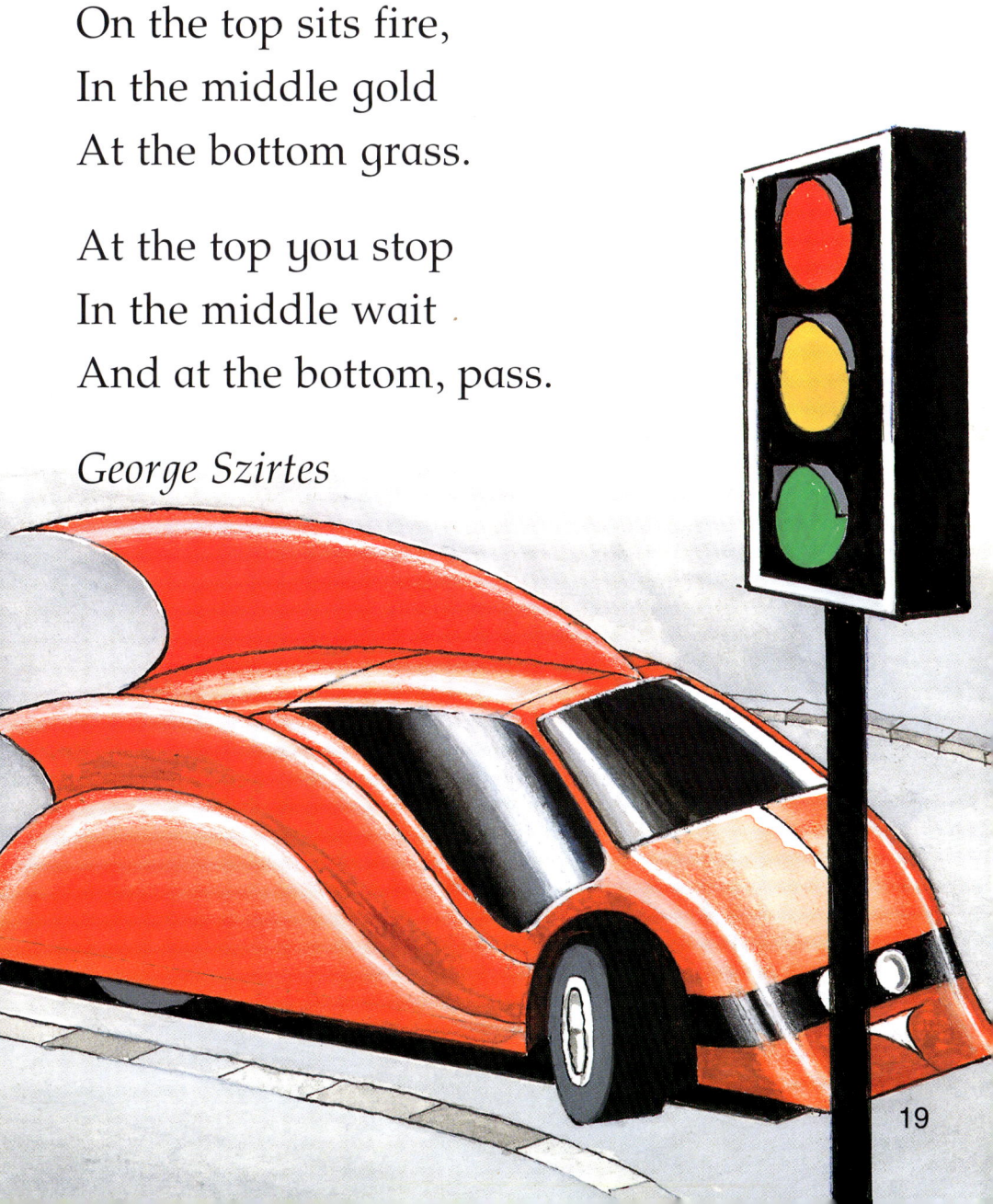

Fishing

There is a fine line

between fishing
and standing
on the bank
like an idiot.

Gerard Benson

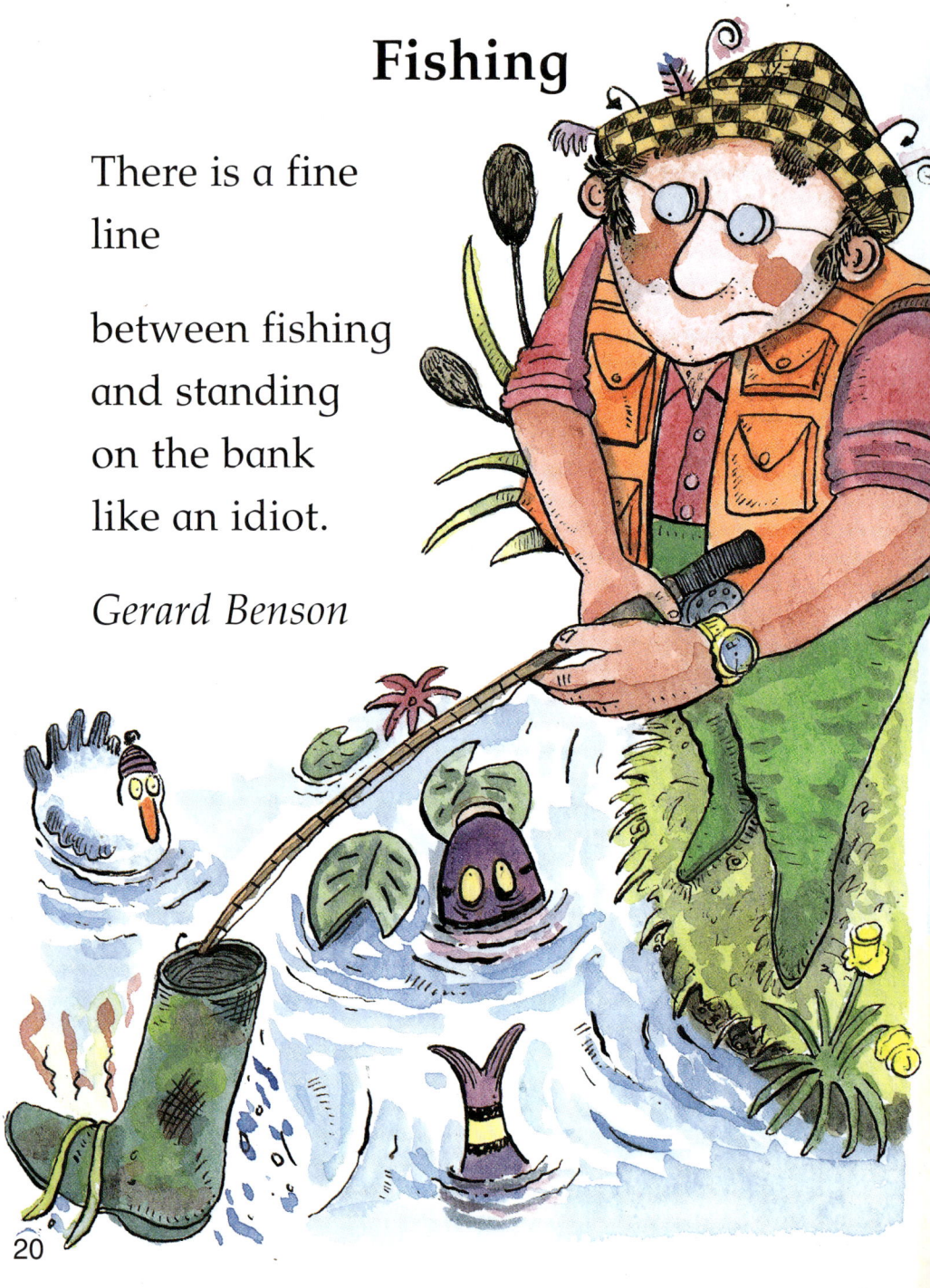

There's an Old Town

There's an old town where nobody goes,
Where nobody lives, where there's never
   a noise.
We pass through it in motors, above it
   in planes,
We clatter right past it in the safety
   of trains.
There's no milkman, no postman,
   no policeman either,
No schoolyard, or playground, not even
   a teacher.
Few people go there and none come away,
There's no one to play with at the end
   of the day.
In it are angels and demons and stones
That lean close together and whisper
   of bones.

Brian Patten

Robber J. Badguy

Robber J. Badguy
Was robbing a bank,
His manners were mean
And his underwear stank.

The neighbours got angry
As grizzly bears,
Bumped him and thumped him
And threw him downstairs.

Dennis Lee

Index of poem features

Dramatic dialogue 6–9, 15

Free verse 4, 12, 20

Haiku 18

Narrative poems 2, 6–9

Patterned language 5, 11, 13, 15, 17, 19, 21
Performance poems 6–9

Rhyming verse 2, 3, 6–9, 10, 11, 14, 15, 21, 22–23

Shape poems 4, 5
Stanzas 6–9, 10, 11, 19, 22–23

Word play 10, 13, 16, 17, 18, 20